PASTOR POTTER'S POINTS

Ellis Potter

Published by: Destinée Media
www.destineemedia.com

Cover and interior by Istvan Szabo, Ifj.
Formatting by Istvan Szabo, Ifj.

Table of Contents

Introduction

This book began with daily emails to the Church where I pastor in Lausanne, Switzerland, during the Corona virus shutdown of 2020 when we could not meet in person. Each email had Bible passages for reading together and a pastoral thought or point, which have been collected to make this book.

These points are mostly original with me and some I have read and adapted, adding my own angle or application. They can be used as a daily dose for meditation or for group discussions in any order or grouping you choose.

The book is 100 points in 100 words on 100 pages. You can read one page each day for over three months and then start over.

The points are uneven in their importance, breadth, and depth. Depending on your condition and situation, some of the "lesser" points might be most important.

The points are very brief and much more needs to be said about them. They are starting points.

The points are compressed to fit into one paragraph of about 100 words each. They need to be read like a prose poem or extended Haiku.

Many of these points were developed because of questions people asked. Some of the points will be familiar or obvious to you. Some might be new.

Not everyone will agree with all the points. Do not stress, just think and pray about them. Or write a better point on the same topic. Many of the points are based on Bible study but the references are not always given as there are often too many. The points are Biblical but not very denominational or political in orientation.

Some of these points are found in the content of my other books.

Ellis Potter, Basel 2020

Abundant Life

If you would ask 10 people at random whether their life would get larger or smaller if they became a Christian what do you think they would say? Some Christians think they can keep their lives pure by avoiding most literature, music and cinema. The Apostle Paul did that when he was legalistic. When he became a Christian, he was free to read and memorize the Greek pagan poets and even quoted a hymn to Zeus in his sermon in Athens (Acts 17). May God help us to love our neighbors by learning about what is in their minds and hearts. Amen.

Apologetics as Love

People need to know the Gospel is the only fully rational and accurate way to understand reality. More deeply they need to be freed from blindness and able to see their own sin and need for God. Our apologetics should be motivated by love and aim at encouraging people toward this freedom. May God help us be prepared to give an answer and soften our hearts to love those we answer. Amen.

Art

Art is artificial, made by the arm of people. Natural things and events can be very pleasing and inspiring, but they are never art. Art is Deliberate Human Action and is responsible. Art is what people do with nature in agriculture, painting, music, cooking, dancing, architectture, etc. Art is responsible dominion over nature. Art is expressions and statements by people. The point is what they say, not whether we like it. Art is not for consumption but for relationships and dialogue. We dehumanize art when we commodify it. Art is not about me but about us. Join the conversation.

Ascension Day

On Ascension Day we remember that Jesus was taken up and a cloud hid Him. This cloud was not water vapor but the Shekinah Glory of God. Jesus went into dimensions of reality which we cannot see but He did not go far away. He had said two things that fit together: "I am going away." and "I am always with you.". Heaven is the supernatural dimensions of reality, which are in the same place as the natural dimensions like height is in the same place as length and width. Jesus is ascended and right here with us. May God use the presence of Jesus to comfort and challenge us. Amen.

Assurance of Salvation

People who belong to God through Jesus Christ are saved and secure even if they are crippled physically or psychology-ically. Salvation does not depend on what we feel about Jesus but on what He has done for us and His power to keep us. Our mood or physical condition is not a good measure of our relationship with God and our growth as His child. A better measure is whether we are grow-ing or shrinking in the fruits of the Spirit: Love, Joy, Peace, Patience, Kindness, Goodness, Faithfulness, Gentleness and Self-Control. May God protect us from being discouraged by our discourage-ments. Amen.

A time, times and half a time

In Revelation 12:14 we read that the Church flees to the desert, where she is taken care of for a time, times and half a time. This adds up to three and a half, which is half of seven. Seven means perfect or complete in Biblical symbolism. John wrote Revelation not long after the crucifixion of Jesus. Can this mean that half of human history happened before Jesus and half will happen after? Did Jesus come to die for everyone right in the middle of human history? Jesus is the center of everything.

Authenticity

Authentic means genuine or honest. More deeply it means coming from the self as in autograph or autobiography. Only God comes from Himself. Everyone and everything else begins with God and not the self. If anything or anyone is "self-referential" it has no meaning because meaning means relationships. Since God is the SELF that causes everything there is no true meaning except in relation to Him. May God help us to take off the pressure to invent ourselves and put it on Jesus, Who can bear it and deal with it perfectly. Amen. Receive your true self from Jesus.

Authority

Authority is the power to describe reality as an author describes a book. All authority comes from God, the author of reality. As children need parents to describe the reality of bedtime, diet and where to play safely, we need God to describe reality to us. He does this in the Bible and by the Holy Spirit. Authority functions in the relationships of God/people, parents/children, government/citizens, husbands/wives, employers/ employees, elders/members of Churches and others. All the relationships are distorted by sin. Freedom comes from working and praying to correct the relationships, not eliminating authority. Pray for those who have authority.

Baptism Testimony

I believe that God; Father, Son and Holy Spirit, has made the world and me and I did not make myself.

I have rebelled against God and tried to make myself according to my ideas and desires. This self-creation cannot be sustained and so it is dead.

I believe Jesus Christ has come into the world and died on the cross so I might have life again.

I have accepted this new life with thanks and am resolved to live as God intends me to live with His help.

Bible Principles and Applications

Many people ask if the Bible is "relevant" today. The principles of the Bible are eternally true. The applications of the principles are culturally specific. For instance, Jesus taught His disciples to wash each other's feet. The principle behind this is humble, practical daily service. In most Churches today foot washing has been reduced to an annual ceremony, so the principle is lost. A better application today would be "wash each other's dishes.". We should not ask how the Bible is relevant to our culture but how our culture is relevant to the Bible. Don't fit the Bible into your life. Fit your life into the Bible.

Blessing and Cursing

Bless means to make life larger, fuller, richer. Curse means to make life smaller. They can be statements or rituals but are much more. Blessing can be money, health, knowledge, encouragement, help, rebukes, and challenges to be better. Blessings make us real. Curses make us unreal. Blessings are often painful while curses are often pleasurable. The dentist is an example of a painful blessing. Flattery is an example of an enjoyable curse. Blessings move us to engage with life and growth. Curses distract us from life and encourage us to shrink.

Choose Life!

Life is hard and complicated; death is easy and simple. Choose life! We can choose death but we don't have to; it will happen to us naturally. But we do have to choose life. Life is hard, death is easy. Our natural life just happens "naturally" but our spiritual life (complete life) must be received from God, chosen and lived. Life is possible because of the death and resurrection of Jesus Christ. We cannot make life. Only God makes life. We only need to receive it from Him. Make life a habit. Be thankful. God bless you.

Christian Listening and Reading

Christians have sometimes been careless readers and listeners from the very beginning. In John 21:22-23 Jesus asked Peter what difference it would make to him if John never died until Jesus returned. People began to say John would never die. It is exciting and dramatic to say this kind of thing, but it can lead to confusion, disappointment, and tensions. Take care to read and hear what is actually there rather than what gives a thrill or proves your point. God help us to be humble and disciplined in our reading, hearing, and speaking. Amen.

Confession

Confessing our sins, specific and general, and getting God's forgiveness and cleansing are essential for the Christian life. Remember each day to bring your sins, known and unknown, to God for forgiveness and cleansing by the blood of Jesus. This clears out the clogging garbage of our lives and gives us a fresh start. It makes us more able to receive God's blessing, guidance and empowerment to serve and bless others. When God has forgiven you, forgive yourself and move on. Don't hang on to false guilt. Make this a daily habit, alone or with others.

Confidence and Trust

In times of crises and stress like the Coronavirus pandemic of 2020, it is hard to trust. Governments make mistakes, anyone we meet might infect us, those who control our online life have various agendas. We cannot see or understand all details. But we can see the big picture in God's Person and promises. He promises to keep us so nothing can separate us from Him. All the confusing and stressful details of our lives have their true meaning in the perspective of God's eternal promises. Keep your eyes on Jesus. Think about His power and faithfulness and be at peace.

Cool

Cool communication is emotional and experiential and does not invite discussion. It is neither true nor false – just cool. Cool expresses taste, which is not debatable. (de gustibus non est disputandum). Cool flies beneath the radar of logic and invites participation without decision making or commitment. It is useful for advertising and propaganda. Hot communication contains content that is definite, committed and either true or false. It invites discussion and decision making. The Gospel of Jesus Christ is hot communication, presenting categories of reality that are either right or wrong and invite a decision. Jesus is not cool.

Cups of Cold Water

Giving a cup of cold water to a little one in Jesus brings rewards. Little ones are around us always, especially when people's lives are reduced and isolated. There are many kinds of cups of cold water: an email, a phone call, an encouragement, shopping, a visit or help with the budget so as to have more control over finances in uncertain times. The Lord will show you what kinds of cups are yours to give. Give as many as possible with joy and invest in your eternal treasure and crown. You will be glad forever.

Death

Death is basically alienation or separation. People are bundles of life with mind, will, emotions, and body all held together by a glue called the soul. If you lose your soul, you lose the glue and fall apart. What makes the glue sticky is the blood of Jesus that cleans the person and keeps them together in life. Physical death is a separation of the parts but people who have the blood of Jesus get put together again forever at the resurrection. We also experience death of relationships, trust, hope, and ideas. Look to Jesus for victory over death.

Evil

Good and evil are not equal opposites. Good is original and evil is a distortion or counterfeit. Evil cannot exist without good but good exists without evil. Evil appears in ways we fear and hate. Evil is more dangerous when it is attractive to us. Evil attracts us to participate in it and take it inside ourselves, so we become evil. Evil is rejecting what God gives us and trying to invent ourselves according to our own imagination. Evil was defeated and swallowed up in victory on the Cross. Lead us not into temptation but deliver us from evil.

Extra Commandments

Thou Shalt have fun – spectacle

Thou Shalt let it all hang out

Thou Shalt go with the flow

Thou Shalt express Thyself

Thou Shalt have a good self-image

Thou Shalt go for the gusto

Thou Shalt be happy

Thou Shalt get in touch with Thy feelings

Thou Shalt be Natural

Felt Needs

Many pastors have been taught to preach to the "felt needs" of the people. They are naturally more popular if they do that. Should we expect people's feelings to correspond to what they actually need in God's Kingdom? Or, should we look into the Bible to find out what God says people need? The first approach is natural. The second approach is spiritual. We don't need an us shaped Jesus. We need a Jesus shaped us. God, help us to want what You want. Amen.

Focus

Many things, people and circumstances invite (tempt) us to concentrate on them. Some urgent things fill the whole screen of our awareness and blot out most else. When our attention is centered on a particular need, fear or hope the picture is always out of focus and distorted. When our attention is centered on Jesus all the particular things come into clear focus. Jesus gives clear meaning and purpose to everything in our lives. If we focus on His Word as on a light at the end of a dark tunnel we know where we are and where we are going.

Forgiveness

Forgive means to "give for", to pay for something someone else owes. If someone hurts us or gossips about us, they cannot possibly pay the debt. The only possibility is that we pay it for them, drawing on the Bank of Jesus, Who paid everything for everyone. It is thought to be therapeutic to forgive to separate from a negative tie. This is not Christian forgiveness. We don't need Jesus to forgive us in order to separate from us. Forgiveness is for healing and restoration of relationships. True forgiveness is impossible without faith in God, Who makes forgiveness possible.

Full Time Christians

Many Christians speak of going into "full time Christian work.". More recently people say, "go into Ministry.". Christians should always be full time Christians and in ministry or service in various ways. All of us are prophets, priests and kings. Whether our funding comes from tithe money or from the local economy does not make a big difference. There is no class system in Christianity and no part time Christian. We should all take responsibility for service and full time Christian life. Be a full time Christian plumber or pastor. Be all you can be for Jesus.

Generational Cursing

Some people have a cloud on their hearts because a grandparent was a witch or a murderer. They think of Exodus 20:5: "…punishing the children for the sin of the fathers to the third and fourth generation.". They miss the last words "of those who hate me.". The question is not what your ancestors did but whether you love the Lord. The consequences of sins (poverty, bad name, ruined ecology) pass on to future generations, but not the guilt. Ezekiel Chapter 18 is full of clarity and comfort on this subject. God help us to live by Your mercy. Amen.

Gifts and Fruits

From the Holy Spirit we have gifts and fruits. The fruits are normative while the gifts are not. Different Christians have different gifts. If you are missing some of the gifts; if you have never spoken in tongues or raised anyone from the dead, your life can still be a normal Christian life. If you are missing any of the fruits (Love, Joy, Peace, Patience, Kindness, Goodness, Faithfulness, Gentleness and Self-control) your life is sub-normal. All the fruits are for each and every Christian. The fruits are a better way of taking your spiritual temperature than the gifts. May God help us to strengthen the fruits that are weak. Amen.

Glory

Glory means weight, solid foundation, dependable. It also means radiant and shining. God is Love. Love is the foundation of all reality and everything has meaning in Love. The Glory of God is Love. We should tell God that He is Glorious, proclaim it to the world and sing about it. When we grow in Love for each other and for the needy world, we show God's Love and magnify His Name. We participate in the coming of His Kingdom here on earth. "Your Kingdom come your Will be done, on earth as it is in heaven." Amen.

God alone is God
and God is not alone

This is only true of the God of the Bible. Buddha alone is Buddha…. Krishna alone is Krishna…. Allah alone is Allah…. All are alone in the beginning. The Christian God is authentically a God of love and relationships because He is three Persons eternally. God is three Persons. The devil is one person. Three persons are other centered. One person is necessarily self-centered as there is no other. One is imploding and dead. Three is radiant and alive. Choose the living God of the Bible for life and love forever.

God is Green

Many people think God is brown, preparing to burn up His creation and not caring about it in the meantime. The "end" is near, in English, can mean the termination is near or the goal is near. In Greek "telos" only means goal. The goal is the cleansing and renewing of creation, not its destruction. "The end is near" actually means "the beginning is near.". God gave humans the power to take care of His creation, not to exploit it and damage it. Christians and green people need to learn that no one is greener than God.

God is Love

It is important not to think or say, "Love is God". That will lead us to worship whatever impermanent idea or experience we consider love. Love cannot be separated from Truth or Justice. Love is not an emotion but a series of actions that encourage and support the beloved in being who God wants them to be. Love can be gentle or violent, encouraging or rebuking. Love must be free to work independently from our feelings. If we act in love and prayerfully our feelings will come into focus. We need God to teach us how to love.

Godly Sorrow and Mourning

Godly sorrow involves repentance and leads to change. It is sorrow that we are not living our life as God wants us to, which we could do. There are elements of joy and thankfulness in it. Worldly sorrow happens to everyone and might lead nowhere. Godly sorrow is a gift and leads to life. "Blessed are those who mourn" is about those who mourn for their sins and the evil in the world, who are sad because they have offended God. It is about Christians in the Kingdom of God, not about any person who grieves over loss or suffering.

Growing Pains

Is there growth of any kind without pain?
When we grow physically, emotionally,
intellectually, socially or in holiness the
old us dies and the new us comes into
being. The old us is familiar. The new us
is unknown so we don't know what we
will be like. We need to walk by faith in
the dark, so we need to take the hand of
Jesus and trust the light of Scripture.
When you have pain, look for the area of
growth. If you find it some pain will
remain, but it will have meaning and
purpose.

Guidance

God's Will is perfect, and He wants us to make responsible choices. Christians make two kinds of mistakes when making decisions: 1. Making them all on our own without any reference to God. 2. Expecting God to tell us exactly what to do so we can blame Him if anything goes wrong. If we say "God told me" no one can discuss our decision with us without arguing with God. There are no perfect choices, only responsible ones. God guides us through Scripture, visions, dreams, finances, words of other people, circumstances and more. We are also free and responsible.

Guilt and Hope

Without guilt there is no hope. Guilt is very unpopular and politically incorrect in our days. People are encouraged to ignore and suppress their feelings of guilt. This might give some relief. If we are not guilty, we are only innocent victims of our circumstances and need to be compensated, understood, accepted and tolerated. People might promise to do that, but no one is able. If we are guilty, we need to be forgiven and restored. Someone is promising to do that. If we bring our broken selves to God through Jesus Christ, we have true hope for the future.

Healing

Healing is a feature of Christianity in the Bible and through the history of the Church. We are all broken and sick and God wants to heal our bodies, our emotions, our minds and our attitudes. Physical healing is a part of our total healing that will happen when Jesus appears. If our bodies are healed and our hearts are not, we lose. If our hearts are healed and our bodies are not, we win. Physical healing is a patch up job because we will die eventually. Healing of our hearts is permanent and eternal.

Heaven on Earth

Jesus taught us to pray "Your Kingdom come, Your Will be done, on Earth as it is in Heaven." Jesus wants the supernatural dimensions of Heaven to come to us here, not for us to go "there". Our true and eternal citizenship is in Heaven, but we won't go there to get it. It will come here when Jesus appears again. Christianity is not a life through escape but through engagement. Suffering and confusion have made Christians think of God taking us someplace else, rather than coming to be with us here. Let's come into focus with God's plan.

Hiding from God

Adam and Eve hid from God among the trees of the garden. People hide from the Creator in the creation behind science or evolution. People hide from God in their pride or their entitlements or their victimhood. People believe they know about good and evil from themselves and can declare themselves innocent. We who believe in Jesus can also hide from Him in a mistrusting cover up of shame. When we hide, we cannot be forgiven, healed and transformed. Let us be transparent with God and trust Him completely. Our only true hiding place is actually God.

Humility and Meekness

Many think of meekness or humility as shyness, always sitting in the back row or being a doormat. Moses was the leader of over a million people and opposed Pharaoh to his face, yet he was "the meekest man alive". When Moses told God he wasn't the right man to lead Israel he was being proud. When he accepted the leadership he was being humble. Meekness is realism about our weak unworthiness and acceptance of what God gives us to do. Meekness is following God rather than our own imagination, fears and desires. The meek will inherit the earth.

Identity

Id-entity. Self-thing. This is not enough for life in God's Kingdom. The identity of Jesus is in His relationships with the Father and the Holy Spirit. Our identity is in our relationships with God and each other. True identity is larger than self. The image of God is them, not him or her. Identify yourself by love rather than a description of yourself. God, please help us to realize our identity is not in ourselves but in our relationships made possible and sustained by You. Amen.

Judgement

Judgement is for correction or destruction. To judge is to make right or fitting and belonging. We don't fit with God because our sins have misshapen us. God's judgment restores our proper shape. The process can be painful and frightening, and we accept it by faith, trusting in God. Those who accept God's salvation through Jesus Christ are blessed by His judgment and made whole and perfect. Those who reject God's salvation are destroyed by His judgment. The refining fire purifies or burns up. Lord, help us to receive your loving judgment and healing. Amen.

Justice and Mercy

Justice by itself means to have what is fair or equal. People think of it as getting what they deserve. This is actually not so positive because if we are sinners what we deserve is death. People are interested in having their rights. If we are sinners, what are our rights? Our only right is to die because the wages of sin is death. Wonderfully, God does not offer us justice or our rights. He offers us mercy and life. Anyone who thinks they deserve salvation probably won't get it. Be poor in spirit and trust God.

Knowing Jesus

Knowing Jesus includes right teaching and information about Him and experience of or with Him through obedience and imitation. Some people get a lot of information about Jesus but don't experience much healing or change. Some people have a lot of experiences with Jesus but don't really know much about Him. It is easy to figure out which side we lean on. A healthy Christian life involves gently leaning on the more neglected side. God bless us and guide us and make our lives more complete. Amen.

Language I

God speaks and is faithful to what He says. People made in His image are intended to speak and be faithful to what they say. When we lose our respect for language and our commitment to the meaning of words, we depend more on facial expressions, body language, emotional energy, social associations and our own appetites for communication. This process feels good and is attractive because it is more relaxed than diligence and commitment. While nonverbal elements of communication are valid, this process also makes us more like animals and less like God. Be careful. Choose life.

Language II

God's Word is faithful and committed and worth keeping. Because we are made in His image our words should also be faithful and committed and worth keeping. It is no help to us if Jesus says, *"Your sins are like forgiven or whatever…"* We have a strong natural sense of an excessive freedom in our use of language (*it is only words*). The Holy Spirit gives us a spiritual sense of commitment and trustworthiness in language. It is a great battle to be faithful and careful with our language because our language sins have become habits. Take courage!

Leaders and Followers

In the Evangelical world there is a great emphasis on leadership with many books and conferences about it. There are always, of course, more followers than leaders. The quality of the followers is at least as important as the quality of the leaders. Followers should support and encourage leaders, expect much and complain little, test everything, pray for the leaders, avoid gossip like the plague, respond to teaching so the leaders are encouraged to teach better, pray and work to be part of the solution rather than part of the problem. Each follower is needed and important. May God help all followers to take their role seriously. Amen.

Let your eye be single

In Matthew 6:19-24 Jesus gave two examples of a divided reality: Storing up treasure on earth or in heaven and serving two masters, God or money. In between these examples is the solution to the problem. If your eye is single, if you see reality as a whole, held together by the power of the Word of Jesus, instead of divided, you will be full of light. If your eye is evil you will see reality as divided and in conflict. May God help us to see a reality unified in His Truth and Love. Amen.

Meditation

Meditation is nonlinear cognitive activity. It works in a sphere or force field. Non-Christian meditation centers on the self and doesn't go anywhere. Biblical meditation is more passive than thought or prayer. It is being open to insights about God and life from the Holy Spirit and the Bible. It focuses on parts of God's character like His unfailing love or infinite power, which are mysterious and cannot be understood completely by the rational mind. Other forms of meditation can be therapeutic in limited ways. Christian meditation is connected to prayer and part of a full life in Christ.

Mother's Day

This should be a lifestyle, not an event. One of the 10 commandments says, "Honor your father and mother.". This does not mean obey as some think. Obeying a senile or demented parent doesn't help anyone. To honor means to respect the life; to support, protect and preserve the life. This is why the commandment is connected to the promise; "so that you will live long.". If your children see you honoring the lives of your parents they will honor your life. Parents can reasonably include other older people, which will increase the social capital and blessing of a nation greatly.

Naturalism

Naturalism is the belief that only matter exists and that everything can be understood and expressed by mathematics. Information is a problem for naturalists. Everyone believes in information and its control over matter, particularly genetic material. Although information controls matter there is no evidence that matter produces information. The religious or faith hypothesis about this fact is that matter does produce information and we have not discovered how yet. The more scientific hypothesis is that information is supernatural. In the beginning was information or relationships which come from a trinitarian and relational God. Matter is created, not self-begotten.

Need

Independence is a basic value of our time. We are taught that we can invent ourselves and be anything we want to be. It is a widespread principle that we should not marry someone if we need them. We should be independent and self-sufficient. This results in people not valuing each other and coming to despise each other after the fun wears off. God made people to need each other, especially in marriage. Christians should identify clear areas of need and thank God when He supplies that need through the person they marry. May God help us to serve and depend on each other. Amen.

News and Propaganda

We need news to inform us and propaganda to motivate us. News is neutral facts. Propaganda is advocacy. News and Propaganda are usually combined. If all news becomes advocacy or propaganda the people have less and less in common. Propaganda can be honest or dishonest. Evangelism should be honest propaganda advocating a worldview and promoting the Kingdom of God. If we pay for news that is mostly propaganda, we get what we pay for and distort truth and culture. Stay awake and test everything.

Our Crown of Glory

Christians look forward to receiving a crown of reward and glory from God. In I Thessalonians 2:19-20 Paul shows us that our crown, glory and joy is other people. The growth of life and beauty in other people that results from our serving them will be our joy forever in the presence of Jesus. If I am your eternal crown, you will want to take very good care of me – to protect me, polish me and perhaps bang the dents out of me. You are my reward and I am your reward. God help us to remember that. Amen.

Peace

Peace or Shalom is not a lack of conflict. It is the foundation and framework of reality given by God for meaning and stability in conflict. If people see conflict in the context of eternity and God's Truth, they will have a more realistic perspective, avoiding prejudice and selfishness. Peace must function in reality rather than in romantic fantasy. If Christians truly act as salt and light in the world, peace will increase. Pray for the Peace of God (Je ru salem).

Pentecost I

Pentecost is the 50th. day after Easter when the Holy Spirit came with new and special power on believers in Jesus to speak to others about God and be understood in every language. God is Love. The power of the Holy Spirit enables us to live in loving relationships and community. The gifts of the Holy Spirit are for serving others. Spirit is wind. The Holy Spirit blows on us and in us to proclaim Jesus and gives us gifts to help us bless others, particularly through teaching them about Jesus, and God's loving salvation. He teaches us how we need to change and be healed.

Pentecost II

The Holy Spirit is the Spirit of Christ Who enters us and bears fruit – love, joy, peace, patience, kindness, goodness, faithfulness, gentleness, and self-control. Christians have different and special gifts. Normally all Christians increase in all the fruits. By these fruits we can measure our growth as God's children and be comforted about our salvation. The Holy Spirit teaches us to pray and ask for what God wants us to have. Pray to the Father in the Name of the Son, through the power of the Holy Spirit. Amen.

Personal

By personal most people mean the self. Biblically it includes the other. God is a Personal God. He is not a Person but three Persons. He is Personal because of His relationships before the beginning of time. The image of God is "them". Everything else in the creation was good but it was not good for Adam to be alone because God is not alone. Jesus is a Personal Savior because He is personal and He saves, not because I personally believe in Him. Personal doesn't begin with me. It begins with God Who is Love. Trust in Him.

Postmodern 10 Commandments
(On two Samsung tablets)

I. Thou shalt value only that which contributes to the flourishing of thy life as thou seeist it.

II. Thou shalt not honor or serve any person, institution, or values other than thyself.

III. Thou shalt not submit to any linguistic conventions that are in any way offensive to thyself at any moment.

IV. Thou shalt order the schedule and rhythm of thy life only according to thy feelings about it.

V. Thou shalt honor thyself and thy convenience above all other people.

VI. Thou shalt accept any collateral damage from the project of thy life.

VII. Thou shalt never be unfaithful to thy own feelings and desires.

VIII. Thou shalt appropriate anything thou canst get away with.

IX. Thou shalt shape truth to serve thyself or whatever.

X. Thou shalt not desire to appropriate any value that cometh not from thine inner self.

Post Modern Beatitudes

1. Blessed are the self-confident for they will succeed.

2. Blessed are those who avoid guilt feelings for they are comforted.

3. Blessed are those with a positive self-image for they will feel better.

4. Blessed are those who clarify their values for they will invent themselves.

5. Blessed are those who know their rights for they will realize their entitlements.

6. Blessed are those who are non-stick surfaced for they will be admired.

7. Blessed are those who mob and gossip for they will move forward.

8. Blessed are those who are politically correct for they will avoid controversy.

Pray Constantly

How do we pray constantly? If we talk to God all the time, we can never talk to anyone else. Perhaps this situation is like at school or work. We don't talk to the teacher or the boss all the time, but they are in the room and everything we do is somehow related to them. They are a reference and guide for us. God is always in the room and He is the Boss. All of our thinking, acting and inter-acting can be in reference to God and have a solid and eternal meaning.

Pray in Jesus' Name

Jesus promised anything we ask God in His Name will be given to us. "Name" isn't a label or a magic word. It means the nature and character and will of Jesus. If we ask for whatever we imagine would be good and add Jesus' name to the prayer the promise is not valid. Praying in His Name means praying for what He wants for us. Why would God give us something He doesn't want us to have? It would not bless us. The goal of praying is to relate to God and be more like Jesus.

Prayer I

Prayer is special and ordinary. It is special and wonderful to be able to speak to the Creator of the Universe and know that He hears us and cares about us and what we say to Him. Prayer is ordinary because we can pray at any moment of the day or night for two seconds or two minutes. We can pray in the middle of working or a conversation or reading or driving (maybe don't close your eyes). Prayer is ordinary because it brings order into our lives in both time and eternity. Prayer is essential for life.

Prayer II

Prayer is not meditation, contemplation, thinking, imagining, feeling, action or work, communion with nature, ecstatic or transcendental experience, Union with the "ALL", silence ritual or magic. Prayer is not natural but is given by God as part of our full spiritual life with Him. Prayer is personal communication between one person and another Person. Prayer is language – direct, definite, and committed. In the Bible God's people speak to Him in ordinary language. God speaks to us through His Word and creation. We can respond by speaking to Him about His Word that brings us life. Return to God. Bring words with you.

Prophets, Priests and Kings

Not many Christians think of themselves as prophets, priests or kings. A prophet tells God's Truth; past, present or future. A priest is a bridge builder making a connection between people and God by prayer. A king gives order and guidelines and makes judgements about what is around. We know that Jesus is Prophet, Priest and King. When we believe in Jesus and belong to Him we take on those roles in the world around us; in our families, our friendships, our workplace, our Churches and communities. This is God's calling for Christians in the world.

Reading the Bible

Reading the Bible every day is important because it keeps us in focus with God's Kingdom and Reality. It is a window into God's stable Truth that works as an anchor for us during days that might otherwise be confusing and out of focus. It also keeps us connected with others who read the same passages, even at a distance. The benefit of reading doesn't depend on our perfectly understanding everything we read. May God give us an appetite for His Word. Amen.

Reality I

Reality is who God is, what He does and what He wants. God is original and infinitely powerful to sustain this reality and make us healthy and happy in it. If we try to live in a reality made by people, past or present, we imitate the serpent/devil, who rebelled and tried to make his own reality, which results in death. We are attracted to a false reality because we believe the myth that in it we will be autonomous and authentic. May God help us to learn about reality from His Word and give us the wisdom and power to choose life. Amen.

Reality II

Reality is Who God is, What He does and What He wants. God is the original reality. He made the universe, which is also real. He made you and me and we are real in His original design and desire. We become unreal by turning away from God and refusing to accept the saving and sustaining of our reality by Him. The devil became unreal through rebellion and tries to draw us into his unreality. Sin, distortion, sickness, alienation and death are all unrealities that war against us to destroy us. Turn to Jesus and get real!

Salt and Light

The world is the salt and light of the Church. Jesus said the opposite in the Sermon on the Mount. Jesus wants the Church to be the clarity and flavor of the world. It is often the other way around. The values of the world – success, relevance, market share, political correctness and social acceptance often get more attention than the values of the Kingdom of God – the fruits of the Spirit and faithfulness to His Word. Christians should be original and different in making culture, not just follow the world around to copy it.

Security

God is Love. God is three Persons. God created everything that is. The foundation of the universe is not matter and energy but love. God loves you. If you receive God's love and remain in it, you are kept and held in the arms of the creator of the universe. You are secure. All other "securities" are temporary and incomplete. In a fallen world many negative things happen to us – accident, sickness, persecution, unemployment, alienation and finally death. None of these things can make us fundamentally insecure when we belong to God. Receive God's Love and trust in it!

Sin

God is the original uncreated reality. Everything created expressed Who He is in its original form. Trying to change reality according to our own imagination is sin. Sin is trying to be God. God is other centered. The devil became self-centered, which is sin. Moses taught "Do not steal.". Jesus taught "Do not want to steal.". Sin is more an attitude than an act. God is love. Sin is what does not conform to God's Character and Word and is not motivated by love. Life is not possible in alternate realities, so the product of sin is death.

Singleness

God's plan or default program for humans includes marriage, children, productive and creative work, and a healthy body and mind. None of us fits this template perfectly. God calls us in our limitations but not to them. We all have special needs. Our needs are finally fully met only in Jesus. We also need to be aware of each other's brokenness and pray and do something to make it as much better as possible. We don't know the extent of each other's lack of fulfillment, but we should do what we can to help.

Speaking of God

In Isaiah 62:6 we read "You who make mention of the Lord, do not keep silent." Do you mention the Lord by saying "God bless you" to your neighbors, colleagues, grocery clerks, doctors and bankers? Sometimes people have been startled when I did that, but they did not seem offended. People need God's blessing. Try bringing God into your conversations in appropriate, positive and inviting ways. We should be excited rather than embarrassed or shy about the Lord. When you bless people pray for them. God give us grace, courage and wisdom to speak of Him. Amen.

Special and Ordinary

Each of us has special or unique experiences and events in our lives as well as ordinary ones. Special experiences like dreams, visions, healings, large group meetings are encouraging and memorable, usually not repeatable. Ordinary things like discipline, prayer habits, covering people's sins with our love, the basic grid of our worldview give order and structure or a frame to our lives and world. The special and the ordinary are both essential and need to be in focus and coordination with each other. Together they make a whole and clear view of the world and our lives.

Spiritual = Supernatural

Most people believe this equation, that spiritual means invisible, non-physical. The Bible teaches us it is false. The birth and resurrection of Jesus were spiritual and pointedly physical. If the physical birth and resurrection are not spiritual, we have lost Christmas and Easter. Our spiritual lives are physical, intellectual, emotional, relational and supernatural. The spiritual kingdom of God includes a physical, new earth. Jesus died to make us whole and complete. Anything that makes us incomplete or divided is unspiritual. God does not want us to be split into spiritual and non-spiritual parts, but to be whole. Spiritual = Totally Real.

Stereo Vision

Having the mind of Christ includes having a single stereo vision of reality. We can look at events and circumstances we are experiencing as with a microscope. We can also look at the eternal promises of God as with a telescope. Christian vision uses the microscope and telescope at the same time, giving us a true stereo vision. Bring your life into focus with God's eternity and apply God's eternal promises to your life at the same time. Don't switch back and forth. The Holy Spirit gives us clear depth of vision. Ask for it and use it.

Strong and Weak

Each of us has strong points and weak points, strong fruits of the Spirit and weak ones. To strengthen what is already strong is natural. To strengthen what is weak is spiritual. God wants us to strengthen what is weak, so we become whole and holy people. If our knowledge is strong, we should strengthen our experience. If our experience is strong, we should strengthen our knowledge. Strengthening what is weak is a frightening move into the unknown. May God help us to walk by faith and hold the hand of Jesus. Amen.

Take up your Cross

Jesus said, "Whoever wants to be my disciple must deny themselves and take up their cross daily and follow me." Jesus took up His Cross, which was the burden of the sins of others. Our cross is not something that happens to us, it is something we actively take up to carry the burden of others. We are not victims of our cross, we are change agents because we take up our cross. Our cross is not sickness or job loss or earthquake. God presents our cross to us in the people and situations we meet. Take it up.

Taste

"De Gustibus Non Est Disputandum" – Taste is not debatable. Our taste is part of who we are, but it is not safe. If we think something is good because we like it or bad because we don't like it, we worship ourselves and lack truth. Liking something tells us about ourselves, not about the thing itself. Taste is subjective and must be married to objectivity to bring forth life. Two confessions will bring freedom: I like what is unworthy and I don't like what is worthy. Don't trust your taste to teach you truth. If we didn't like sin we would never do it.

Thankfulness

True thankfulness requires humility and poverty of spirit. Thankfulness to God is infinite because when we are thankful for being thankful an upward spiral begins. Thankfulness is always appropriate to God and often to others. If we remember what to be thankful for it puts the other things in perspective with God's Grace. We need to think about bad things in order to resist and forgive. Being thankful refreshes and energizes us and is therapeutic. A small investment in being thankful pays a big dividend in blessing. Make thankfulness, especially in hard times, a joyful discipline in your life.

The Battle

If we teach our children that gender is a gift and not something we choose for ourselves according to our feelings; that we do not invent ourselves and Jesus only is Lord, it will bring our children and us into strong conflict at school and in our culture in general. Our situation as Christians is not safe, but God is with us. The culture around us teaches us and our children deadly, unbiblical ideas and demands that we conform to them. Where should we draw a line and take a stand? May God give us wisdom and courage. Amen.

The Blood of Jesus

In a sinful world covered by the dust of death, we live by the death of others. God has given us animals who have died to give us food, clothing and shelter all through history. The blood of these animals points to the Blood of Jesus, which glues our broken selves and broken world together. Jesus loves us so much He gave His Blood for us so we can have new life and be with Him and each other in God's Kingdom forever. Our lives are precious and beautiful to God. We should take care of ourselves by caring for and serving others.

The Cloud of Glory

The Cloud of God's Glory or Presence is found throughout Scripture and is an interface between the natural and supernatural dimensions. The Cloud helps us understand many events like the burning bush, the Exodus, smoking Mt. Sinai, the tabernacle and temple presence of God, the star of Bethlehem, the Transfiguration, the Ascension, Paul's conversion and the second appearing of Jesus. The Cloud is experienced as fire, light, darkness, or star and is never water vapor. The experience of the Cloud seems to happen while awake and often includes a voice. May God help us to see more of the whole picture. Amen.

The Default Program

God's default program for human life involves marriage and children, good health, productivity, and trust in Him. None of us fit the program fully so there are special programs like singleness, growth through adversity and contentment in limitations. All of us are handicapped. Some of the handicaps are obvious and some are hidden. Some handicaps can be healed during our lifetime and some not. We should be sensitive and sympathetic to our handicaps and those of others. Be realistic and look for God's victory in your handicapped condition. Encourage and support others in their special situations.

The Kingdom of God

Jesus said the Kingdom is near, coming, here, among us and inside us. This does not describe the Church or someplace far away. The Kingdom of God is the rule of God in the world, in our societies and families and in our hearts. "Your Kingdom come" and "Your Will be done" mean the same thing. Jesus wants the rule of God to come on the earth. We should want it with Him. God, help us to want your will and receive it first in our hearts and then reaching out to others. Amen.

The Least Faith

People become Christians because of many reasons, emotions and circumstances. One reason for believing Christianity is that it takes less faith to believe in it than to believe in anything else. Faith is needed but faith like a mustard seed, not faith like a coconut. Our faith can be small but living and growing and bearing fruit because Christianity gives clear answers to more questions than other faith systems. It takes more faith to believe that people are good or evolution or communism or rationalism or materialism or astrology. Choose the rational faith. Choose Christianity.

The Parable of the Banana Peel

If I get up late and am running on the platform to catch a train to the airport to go on a mission, I might slip on a banana peel and break my ankle. How am I to understand the situation? Is it caused by my sin of getting up late? Is it caused by the sin of the banana eater? Is it caused by the devil to prevent people being blessed on the mission? Is it caused by God because the train is going to crash down the track? All things work for good for those who love the Lord. My job is not to figure everything out but to love the Lord and my neighbors.

The Unforgivable Sin

Some Christians worry they might have committed the unforgivable sin, blasphemy against the Holy Spirit, and be permanently separated from God. Sin is acting and speaking but is more deeply an attitude. Blasphemy against the Holy Spirit is the attitude that His work is evil, particularly His testimony about Jesus Christ. People who have this attitude cannot repent and be forgiven because they believe they are right. People who worry about this sin have most probably not done it or they wouldn't care. People who have committed it are satisfied with themselves.

Theology

Theology is the study of God. We need theologians to study, interpret and apply God's Word so we know how to live in His Kingdom. Often theology becomes the study of other theologians. It can get academically disconnected from ordinary life. God is Love. If the study of theology does not lead to greater love of God and other people, it has lost its way. The goal and focus of theological studies must always be the love of God and our neighbors.

Time and Eternity

A matrix is an atmosphere in which things happen. Water is the matrix of tea, air is the matrix of sound, cyber-space is the matrix of emails. The matrix of things happening in space is time. The matrix of things happening outside of space is eternity. Eternity is not infinite time. It is a separate matrix. Every point of time is present to every point of eternity. This is why prophecy is possible. We can connect with eternity through prayer and other means. When Jesus appears time and eternity will conflate in God's Kingdom on the new earth. May God help us to see from His perspective of eternity. Amen.

Total Freedom = Death

In our culture freedom is increasingly valued over form, loyalty, responsibility, dependability, or obedience. People were not made by God to be alone or independent. If we become totally free from our need for each other as individuals or society, we move toward alienation and isolation, which is death. People want to be free in terms of their imagination, but our imagination doesn't produce reality. Reality is Who God is, what He does and what He wants. Freedom is lively and has meaning only with form. God, help us to be free in the forms You give us. Amen.

Traditions

Traditions are essential for remembering God's saving history and identifying ourselves in the flow of history that is larger than our moment. Artistic and cultural expressions happen in traditions. If traditions take first place in our hearts, they can replace the love of God and neighbor and become idols. The Holy Spirit can help us love and profit from our traditions without worshiping them and despising others. Traditions should serve Christ and His Love for the whole world. Christ is not contained in our traditions. Let us humble ourselves so our hearts and minds can be guarded in Christ Jesus our Lord.

Trust

Only God is fully trustworthy and only in His actual character and promises. Our imagination is not trustworthy. Everything and everyone betrays us in small and big ways, so we are wounded and handicapped. Much mental illness is an inability to trust. Being trustworthy is a way of being salt and light in the world. Trust is fragile and easily damaged. Trust in God is healing. When we are consistently faithful in what we say and do we add to the social capital of our culture. Trust is part of the Kingdom of God. Pray and work for it.

Truth and Meaning

Truth does not equal fact. Truth equals fact plus meaning. Meaning means relationships, which means that nothing and no one has meaning in itself. Anything that is only self-referential has no meaning. The meaning of the color red is not in the color red but in its relationships with blue, green, brown, etc. The meaning of Adam at the creation was pointedly not in Adam (it is not good for man to be alone) but in his relationships with God and Eve. The meaning of Jesus is not in Jesus but in His relationships with the Father and the Holy Spirit. Truth is relational.

Truth and Mercy

Some people are tempted by the hope of improving relationships by telling the whole truth. Being fully open and not hiding can feel purifying. But God's Truth is not facts alone. Truth only brings life when it works with Love and Mercy. If the way you blow your nose truly disgusts me, I might choose in mercy not to tell you. The way Truth and Mercy work together is mysterious. We need God's Wisdom to make the best imperfect choice. God help us to be slow to speak and quick to pray. Amen.

Veganism

The main point of veganism is against the commodification of animals: People should not own, exploit, buy or sell animals. Living like this is only possible with the support of modern technology for transportation, agriculture and synthetic fabrics for clothing. The vegan diet is part of the picture. Veganism excludes the owning of animal pets. The big question is whether humans are responsible for organizing the other animals, as the Bible teaches, or humans should live like vegetarian animals without using animals to support civilization. To decide this it is important to know whether nature is perfect or broken.

Victorious Life

Sometimes we are disappointed and discouraged because we are not overcoming various ungodly habits of action and attitude. We are alarmed because we are not increasing in holiness and victory. The real source of our salvation is not in our effort but God's Grace in Jesus Christ. Often God is at work in us in ways we don't see. Check for growth in the fruits of the Spirit. When you find an increase in love, joy, peace, patience, kindness, goodness, faithfulness, gentleness or self-control you will know that God is at work in you and be encouraged to make your own effort.

Victory in Crises

In 2020 we are aware of our need for God to protect and heal us from the Corona Virus and its social and economic side effects. Let us bring our other areas in need of protection and healing to God: our tendency to worry, our groundless fears, our attitudes of prejudice and blame, giving a negative or paranoid interpretation to things people say and do, being a part of the problem instead of part of the solution. If we can be changed and healed in these and other ways, the time of corona will be a time of victory in our lives and relationships.

What about those who have never heard?

Many tender-hearted Christians worry about those who have never heard the Gospel, read the Bible or met a missionary. The basic thing anyone needs to know to be saved is that they are broken and need God to forgive and fix them. God tells everyone this in various ways: The Bible, conscience, dreams, the Holy Spirit's conviction. The question is how people respond. In Romans 1 we read no one has an excuse. It is urgent to give people more opportunities to respond by missionary work near and far. Encourage poverty of spirit.

What is Love?

Love is not an emotion, attachment or appetite. Love is not centered on the self but on the other. The center of Jesus is not Jesus but the Father and the Holy Spirit. The center of the Father and the Holy Spirit is the other two Persons of God. Each Person of God empties Himself into the other two to supply and sustain them. This means that each Person is emptied once and filled twice so there is a constant increase. Love is a series of responsible choices and actions by which we encourage and enable the loved one to be who God made them to be.

Worry

We are commanded not to worry. This is hard because many things threaten, stress and confuse us. We want to know the future and it is hard to trust God about the unknown. When we worry about things, we often feel that we are being more responsible than when we say "no" to worry and trust God. When we trust, we have more energy and stability to be responsible. Wisdom is seeing the difference between things we can actually do something about and things we must passively trust God about. Pray for wisdom. God wants you to have it.

Worship

Worship is "worth ship" or telling someone how much value they have. We worship God or money or advertisers or cultural norms by praising them in word and song, investing in them, imitating them and obeying them. Worship is 24/7. It doesn't stop when the meeting ends. We come to Church for "worship prep", to be prepared to worship on Monday and every day. Our worship of many things is forced and exaggerated. Worship of God is free and can never be exaggerated. We can praise Him whole-heartedly knowing He will never be unworthy of our praise and worship.

CPSIA information can be obtained
at www.ICGtesting.com
Printed in the USA
LVHW081334051020
667964LV00018B/1841

9 781938 367519